Our **WILD**™ **WORLD**
SERIES

Sea Turtles

NORTHWORD
Minnetonka, Minnesota

DEDICATION
In loving memory of my aunt, Anna K. Allman, whose
willing spirit inspired love, compassion, and courage.

Photography © 2000: Doug Perrine/Innerspace Visions: front cover, pp. 9, 10, 14-15, 21, 24-25, 27; Michele
Westmoreland/Danita Delimont, Agent: pp. 4, 12-13; Andre Seale/Innerspace Visions: p. 5; Marilyn Kazmers/SharkSong: pp.
6, 34-35, 40; Jonathan Bird/O.R.G.: pp. 16, 18-19, 42; Erwin & Peggy Bauer/Tom Stack & Associates: pp. 22-23, 45; Peter
Pritchard/Innerspace Visions: pp. 28, 29; Mark Strickland/Innerspace Visions: p. 30; Ingrid Visser/Innerspace Visions: p. 33;
Lynda Richardson/Danita Delimont, Agent: back cover, pp. 38-39, 43.

Front cover photograph: green sea turtle.
Back cover photograph: loggerhead sea turtle.
Illustrations by John F. McGee
Designed by Russell S. Kuepper
Edited by Barbara K. Harold

NorthWord
11571 K-Tel Drive
Minnetonka, MN 55343
www.tnkidsbooks.com

Library of Congress Cataloging-in-Publication Data

Jay, Lorraine A.
   Sea turtles / text by Lorraine A. Jay ; illustrations by John F. McGee.
     p. cm. -- (Our wild world series)
   Summary: Describes the habitat, physical characteristics, behavior, and life cycle of the
seven species of sea turtles, and discusses their endangered status.
   ISBN: 1-55971-746-7 (softcover)
   ISBN 13: 978-1-55971-746-5
   1. Sea turtles--Juvenile literature. [1. Sea turtles. 2. Turtles. 3. Endangered species.]
I. McGee, John F. II. Title. III. Series.
QL666.C536 J38 2000
597.92'8--dc21
                                                              00-028352

Printed in Malaysia

Sea Turtles

Lorraine A. Jay
Illustrations by John F. McGee

NORTHWORD
Minnetonka, Minnesota

Hatchlings!

ONE HUNDRED sea turtles, each no bigger than a baby's hand, scramble from their buried nest. Following instincts that have guided their ancestors for millions of years, the tiny hatchlings scurry across the sand to the sea. When they reach the water, they are tumbled by the waves. Some are tossed onto shore and left stranded on their backs. They wrestle helplessly until another wave rescues them. Back and forth, back and forth, they struggle in the surf. One by one, they disappear into the giant sea.

Where are they going? How many will survive the journey? And, how will they find their way back to this same beach several years from now to lay their own eggs in the sand? These are only some of the questions you might ask about sea turtles. All over the world, scientists are gathering clues to understand these mysterious creatures of the sea and to help them survive.

It is a hard struggle for these young green sea turtles to reach the ocean.

It may take a hatchling several hours to crawl out of its nest buried in the sand.

Under the cover of darkness, a loggerhead
leaves the ocean to lay her eggs in the sand.

Sea turtles are air-breathing reptiles. They swim in the waters off every continent except Antarctica. Like other reptiles, they are cold-blooded animals. They get their body warmth from the sun and the water around them. Coral reefs, sea-grass beds, estuaries, coastal shallows, and the waters of the open ocean are all sea turtle habitats.

Underwater, sea turtles have excellent vision, but out of the water they see only close objects. Looking through water helps their vision the way eyeglass lenses help some people to see.

Sea turtles do not have teeth, but their jaws have sharp edges like a bird's beak. They do have ears, but you can't see them. Their eardrums are covered by skin.

Most sea turtles have hard bony shells. The shell protects their internal organs the same way your rib cage protects you. The upper shell, called the carapace (KAR-uh-pace), is connected by cartilage to the bottom shell, called the plastron (PLAS-tron). The scutes, or plates, on the carapace form a design that helps identify each kind of turtle.

Sea Turtle
FUNFACT:

Adult male and female sea turtles are about the same size, except males have longer, thicker tails and longer claws.

At first glance, sea turtles look like land turtles. But if you take a closer look, you will see some differences. Nearly all land turtles have a high, dome-shaped shell. When a predator comes along, the turtle pulls its legs, head, and tail into its shell and waits. After a while, the predator gives up and searches for an easier meal.

Sea turtles are not so lucky. Their shells are flatter with no space for them to use for hiding. Better suited for life in the sea, their streamlined shells allow them to move through the water with the grace and ease of an Olympic swimmer. Their speed also helps them escape enemies such as hungry sharks. Some sea turtles may even swim as fast as 22 miles (nearly 35 kilometers) per hour!

Sea Turtle　　　　　　**Land Turtle**

Another major difference is that land turtles have legs and webbed feet that they use to swim a kind of "doggy paddle." Sea turtles have 4 powerful flippers. As they swim, they move their front flippers up and down like wings. They seem to be flying through the water. They use their rear flippers and short tail like a boat rudder to help them steer.

The light underside of this green sea turtle works like camouflage with the sky above.

During the day, sea turtles spend most of their time swimming underwater and foraging (FOR-ij-ing), or searching for food. They swim to the surface about every 5 minutes to take a deep breath of air.

A loggerhead uses its powerful jaw muscles to crush shells for the food inside.

Sea turtles sleep at night. While resting or sleeping they need much less oxygen, so some are able to sleep underwater for as long as 5 hours at a time. Finding a good place to sleep is important to keep the turtles from drifting with the current while they are sleeping. They often choose a ledge or reef to protect them from the moving water.

This loggerhead will have a clean shell
thanks to the work of some fishes.

Sea turtles are peaceful creatures. Birds on long flights at sea will sometimes take a rest on the back of a sea turtle. Barnacles and algae (AL-gee) attach to the turtle's shell, and small fish often nibble at the shell, keeping it clean. Sea turtles do not seem to mind giving all of these creatures a free ride.

There are 7 species (SPEE-sees), or kinds, of sea turtles. Each species has its own unique physical appearance and behaviors. Adults of some species are small enough to fit in a kitchen sink; others are too big for a bathtub!

Five species are found in the coastal waters of the United States: green turtles, loggerhead turtles, leatherback turtles, hawksbill turtles, and Kemp's ridley turtles.

Sea Turtle
FUNFACT:

A caliper is the instrument
used to measure the
length of a sea turtle's carapace—
from near the neck to the
edge of the tail.

Sometimes a green turtle shares its resting place
with other sea creatures.

This green has found a tasty meal
on the rocks near shore.

Green turtles are not actually green. Their shells are olive-brown or black. The name refers to the color of their body fat. Young green turtles eat a variety of foods, but change their diet once they've grown to the size of a Frisbee. As adults, they are the only sea turtles that are herbivores (HERB-uh-vorz), or plant eaters. Their diet of algae and sea grass turns their body fat green.

Green turtles can weigh up to 500 pounds (225 kilograms), with a carapace that can grow to be 48 inches (122 centimeters) long.

Greens have long been hunted for their flavorful meat and eggs. Centuries ago during long voyages, sailors hauled live green turtles onto their ship's deck. Flipped over on their backs, the helpless sea turtles were kept fresh and waiting until they were needed for dinner. In some parts of the world they are still hunted as food.

Sea Turtle
FUNFACT:

**Some researchers divide
green sea turtles into
2 separate species:
the Atlantic green and
the Pacific green or black.**

One look at a loggerhead and you will know how it gets its name. Not much smaller than a green, a loggerhead is easily recognized by its log-shaped head that measures about 10 inches (25 centimeters) wide. Loggerheads use their powerful jaw muscles to crush their food. They most often eat clams and crustaceans (krust-A-shuns), such as crabs and spiny lobsters.

The east coast of Florida is a very popular breeding place for loggerheads.

Sea Turtle
FUNFACT:

**Fossils of the earliest
sea turtles date back to
150 million years ago!**

Even with a damaged front flipper,
this loggerhead swims well and forages for food.

Leatherbacks are the largest of all marine reptiles. They can weigh between 650 and 1,300 pounds (290 to 585 kilograms), and grow to 6 feet (1.8 meters) long. One leatherback found along the coast of Wales weighed over 2,000 pounds (900 kilograms) and measured over 9 feet (3 meters) long. Imagine a turtle the size of a sports car!

Leatherbacks get their name because they are the only sea turtle without a hard shell. Their barrel-shaped body is covered by a dark, leathery hide with white spots and long ridges.

Leatherbacks have very long front flippers but no claws. Other sea turtles have one or two claws on each front flipper.

Unlike other reptiles, leatherback sea turtles can regulate their body temperature. This allows them to make exceptionally deep dives and to migrate thousands of miles to and from warm, tropical waters.

Following schools of jellyfish, leatherbacks may forage as far north as Iceland. It takes a lot of jellyfish to feed a leatherback!

This hawksbill turtle moves quickly across the sand by lifting herself on her flippers.

Hawksbills are named for their sharp hawk-like beaks. These turtles can weigh as much as 175 pounds (79 kilograms), and their carapace may grow to 3 feet (1 meter) long. Hawksbills eat a wide variety of foods, but sponges are their favorite. Mysteriously, the tiny glass-like needles on the skin of these marine creatures don't seem to harm the turtles at all.

Many people say that hawksbills would win the prize for beauty. Their lovely black-and-yellow shell is used for making tortoiseshell combs, jewelry, and other ornaments.

Unfortunately, this demand has brought hawksbills to near extinction. In the United States and more than 100 other countries it is now illegal to import, sell, or transport sea turtles or sea turtle products.

Pages 24-25: A coral reef with many sea sponges makes a good feeding place for a hawksbill.

The most endangered sea turtle is the Kemp's ridley. This species was named after Richard Kemp, who helped discover it. Ridleys (Kemp's and olive) are the smallest sea turtles, weighing less than 100 pounds (45 kilograms) and measuring about 24 inches (61 centimeters) long.

These turtles come ashore in large groups and nest in daylight. Scientists call this *la arribada*, which is Spanish for "the arrival." An arribada filmed in 1947 at Rancho Nuevo, Mexico, recorded an estimated 40,000 Kemp's ridleys nesting in one day! Today, the population of nesting females at that same beach is estimated to be about 500.

Sea Turtle
FUNFACT:

So far, there is no sure way
to tell the age of a sea turtle.
Researchers believe that turtles
of some species live to be
20 to 30 years old, while others
may live closer to 80!

The Kemp's ridley is often found in the Gulf of Mexico.
It likes shallow areas with sandy and muddy bottoms.

These olive ridleys are part of a large group coming ashore to nest.

Two species of sea turtles are not found in the coastal waters of the United States: olive ridley turtles and Australian flatback turtles.

The olive ridley was named for the color of its heart-shaped shell. Olive ridleys are found in the tropical waters of the Pacific, the Atlantic, and the Indian oceans. Like the Kemp's ridleys, they also come ashore in daylight to nest in large groups.

Sea Turtle
FUNFACT:

A sea turtle's plastron is usually whitish or yellowish. The carapace is much darker.

The Australian flatback is named for the flatness of its shell. It weighs up to 200 pounds (90 kilograms) and measures about 3 feet (1 meter) long. This is the most easily protected species because flatbacks stay close to home in coastal Australian waters.

Most of what we know about sea turtles we have learned from nesting females and hatchlings. They are the easiest turtles to find and study.

If a nesting turtle like this Australian flatback is disturbed before she begins laying her eggs, she will leave the beach and wait for a safer time. This is called a "false crawl."

Dr. Archie Carr is known as the father of sea turtle research. He dedicated his life to solving the mysteries surrounding them. His enthusiasm has inspired many other scientists to continue his work.

To gather useful information, researchers attach satellite transmitters to some nesting turtles and mark others with identification tags. This helps tell about the turtles' habits and where they go once they leave the beach.

At one time, green sea turtles were among the most plentiful of all sea turtles. Today, they are endangered.

Eleven days after leaving the Florida beach, one loggerhead was recaptured off the coast of Cuba—400 miles (644 kilometers) away. Another loggerhead, tagged on Melbourne Beach, Florida, was recaptured almost 10 months later near the Dominican Republic—about 1,000 miles (1,600 kilometers) away!

From the moment a male sea turtle enters the ocean as a hatchling, he spends all of his life in the sea. But an adult female must leave the ocean to lay her eggs in the sand. If she were to lay her eggs in the water, her young growing inside the shells would not have the oxygen they need, and they would drown.

From what they have learned, scientists believe that a mother sea turtle will return to lay her eggs on the beach where she was born. How does she remember that same beach? She swims through thousands of ocean miles without landmarks to help her. How does she find her way back? Some scientists think she remembers the taste, texture, and smell of the sand from when she was a hatchling. Perhaps the earth's magnetic field affects her internal compass, or maybe the direction of the waves gives her a cue. Scientists are still studying this mystery.

Sea Turtle FUNFACT:

A nesting sea turtle sheds tears, but she is not crying. The tears help to get rid of the extra salt in her body and to wash the sand from her eyes.

Researchers are also trying to find a way to tell how old a female is when she lays her first clutch, or group, of eggs. They know that she usually lays her eggs at least twice during a nesting season. Most species nest every 2 to 3 years.

A mature female will mate with an adult male turtle in the shallows offshore. When she leaves the water to lay her eggs, she usually waits for the darkness of night. The ocean is her home, but she must come ashore. She is very cautious when she touches land. The slightest movement will scare her back to sea.

When she is sure that she is safe, she uses her flippers to drag herself across the sand. Every inch is a challenge. Out of the water, her lungs are squeezed under the weight of her heavy shell. She stops frequently to catch her breath and to check for signs of danger. She struggles forward until she reaches the sand above the high-tide line. The nest site is important. Her eggs must be safe from the ocean tides, so she chooses a spot carefully.

If she is a loggerhead, she will clear a shallow place in the sand. If she is a green, she will spend more time sweeping the sand with her flippers to hollow out a body pit about 15 inches (38 centimeters) deep. By cupping her rear flippers like hands, the mother turtle carves a bottle-shaped hole in the sand behind her. When the egg chamber is completed, she rests.

Sea Turtle
FUNFACT:

Sea turtles leave a trail in the sand that looks a lot like tractor tracks. Each species has its own unique pattern.

Pages 34-35: A female loggerhead clears a nest site with her powerful front flippers.

This green sea turtle is going back to the sea after laying her eggs in the sand. She will never see her hatchlings.

A sea turtle lays a clutch of about 100 eggs, depending on the size of the turtle and the species.

Each egg is about the size of a ping-pong ball. Unlike a chicken egg, it has a tough leathery shell that keeps it from cracking as it drops into the nest. The temperature of the egg in the nest helps determine whether the hatchling is male or female. Warmer temperatures usually produce females, and cooler temperatures produce mostly males.

This is an important fact because as people develop the coastline the nesting beach changes. For example, a high-rise hotel built along the beach will block some of the warmth of the sun by casting a shadow on the sand. The sand will be cooler, and more hatchlings will be males. What an effect that could have on the whole sea turtle population!

When the mother sea turtle finishes laying her eggs, she fills the egg chamber with sand. She moves forward out of the pit, sweeping the sand behind her as she goes. Because she will not stay here to protect her nest, she does her best to hide it from land predators such as dogs, raccoons, skunks, and coyotes. When the nest is covered, her work is done for the night. She circles back to the water and disappears under the waves. She may swim nearby and return in a week or two to nest again, or she may swim hundreds of miles to her favorite feeding grounds.

Sea Turtle
FUNFACT:

An eggshell is full of tiny holes that you cannot see. Even when the egg is buried in the sand, oxygen can pass through the shell to the young inside.

Pages 38-39: These young loggerheads will soon be on their own.

The clutch of eggs incubates in the warm sand. After about 60 days, the eggs begin cracking. Each hatchling waits quietly in the nest until all the eggs crack open. Then, like a team, the hatchlings go into action. Their squirming and thrashing causes the roof and sides of the egg chamber to cave in, and they rise to the surface of the sand!

Together they leave the nest at night or in the early morning when the sand is cool. One hatchling makes a dash to the sea, and all the others follow. They must hurry. Hatchlings are a fast-food meal for hungry gulls, ghost crabs, and other predators!

A leatherback hatchling swims near the surface, making it easy prey for hungry gulls.

How do they find their way to the sea? Scientists believe that hatchlings are attracted to light. At night when the beach is dark, the brightest light is the reflection of the moon and stars on the water. Even on a cloudy night, the turtles move toward the sea.

Scientists have learned that artificial lights shining on the beach can confuse the hatchlings. They will not survive if they go the wrong way. People living near the shore have been asked to help by turning off their outside lights during nesting season. At Kennedy Space Center in Florida, NASA even changed the lighting at the launch pads so hatchlings from the nearby beach would not be confused.

Once they find the ocean, the hatchlings are still not out of danger. Predators in the water, such as barracudas, also have an appetite for hatchlings.

The hatchlings swim toward the horizon for the next day or so, without stopping. Scientists call this the "swim frenzy." No one can say for sure where they go. But, many hatchlings have been found in the floating sargassum seaweed that drifts with the ocean's currents.

Green sea turtle hatchlings leave their nest and scramble toward the sea.

Hatchlings climb aboard and hitch a ride. They hide from predators in the weeds and find food like baby shrimp and jellyfish.

Hatchlings are not picky eaters. They will eat anything that collects in the seaweed, even garbage, tar, and other pollution.

Swept along by the ocean's many currents, hatchlings grow up in the floating sargassum. Scientists believe that during the first year or two, hatchlings that leave the beach in Florida will circle the whole Atlantic Ocean at least once. Then they swim out of the seaweed raft to look for food in other habitats.

Whether they are green turtles grazing in a sea grass pasture, or hawksbills snatching sponges from a coral reef, or loggerheads chasing crabs in a warm lagoon, all sea turtle species are in serious trouble. Scientists estimate that only 1 out of 1,000 hatchlings will survive to adulthood.

After leaving its nest on a Florida beach, a loggerhead hatchling reaches shelter in the drifting sargassum seaweed.

Occasionally, adult sea turtles are attacked by natural predators, such as sharks or killer whales, but humans are their worst enemies.

Sea turtles are hunted for their eggs, meat, and shells. Many turtles drown in fishing nets. Some get sick from ocean pollution, and others die after swallowing trash that they have mistaken for food. A floating plastic bag looks a lot like a jellyfish to a foraging sea turtle!

Learning about sea turtles may be the most important key to saving them. A great way to learn about sea turtles is to take a "turtle walk." During nesting season, turtle walks are conducted by trained volunteers. These volunteers have a special permit that allows them to guide visitors onto nesting beaches. If you are a lucky observer, you will watch a ritual that has been repeated for millions of years.

Sea turtles have outlived the dinosaurs! All over the world, scientists, governments, corporations, and volunteers are working hard to protect these ancient reptiles and to help them survive for centuries to come.

Sea Turtle
FUNFACT:

Some females may nest
many times in a season, laying
hundreds and hundreds of eggs!

Scientists are easily able to identify this Kemp's ridley by its shell design.

Internet Sites

You can find out more interesting information about sea turtles and lots of other wildlife by visiting these Internet sites.

www.animal.discovery.com   Discovery Channel Online

www.cccturtle.org   Caribbean Conservation Corporation

www.kidsplanet.org   Defenders of Wildlife

www.nationalgeographic.com/kids   National Geographic Society

www.nwf.org/kids   National Wildlife Federation

www.seaturtle.org   Seaturtle.org

www.seaturtlespacecoast.org   Sea Turtle Preservation Society

www.worldwildlife.org   World Wildlife Fund

http://nature.org/   The Nature Conservancy

Index

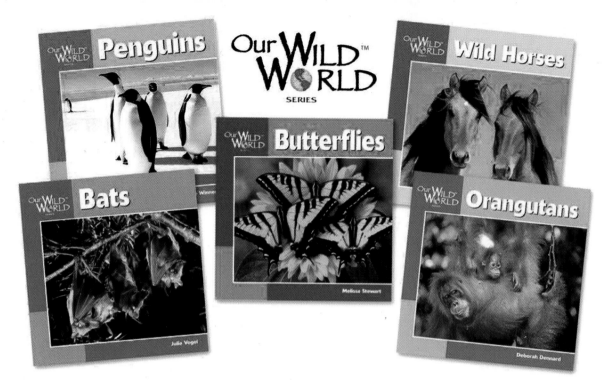

Titles available in the Our Wild World Series:

NorthWord
Minnetonka, Minnesota